IMAGES OF

Lytham
St Annes

IMAGES OF

Lytham St Annes

Evening Gazette

Compiled by
Steve Singleton

The Breedon Books
Publishing Company
Derby

First published in Great Britain by
The Breedon Books Publishing Company Limited
Breedon House, 44 Friar Gate, Derby, DE1 1DA.
1996

ISBN 1 85983

Printed and bound by Butler & Tanner Ltd., Selwood Printing
Works, Caxton Road, Frome, Somerset.
Colour separations by Colour Services, Wigston, Leicester.

Contents

Acknowledgements

The author wishes to express his grateful thanks for the assistance in the publication of this book to fellow postcard collectors Mr Andrew Firth and Mr Gordon Russell. A special thanks go to chief librarian Mrs Glenn Lougher and the girls of the *Gazette* library department, to editorial secretary Mrs Suzanne Steedman and to the *Gazette* photographic department.

How to obtain photographs from this book
Copies of all *Gazette* photographs used in this publication – which are those indicated by a reference number – can be purchased. Contact the *Gazette* photosales department 01253 839999 for details, quoting Images of Lytham St Annes and the reference number shown.

Foreword

by Michael Jack MP

SOMEONE once said that a picture is worth a thousand words. That advice was never more correct in terms of this splendid book which helps to tell the story of a very special part of the Fylde namely Lytham and St Annes.

This photographic record helps underscore the very special characteristics of these two towns. In one sense they are united as they both front on to the Ribble Estuary but in terms of their history they are very separate.

I can well remember in my early days in the area attending an evening meeting in St Annes. One of my audience asked where I had come from. I replied, Lytham. To which there was a response, "Lytham, indeed!" It was then I recognised that in spite of the modern postal address Lytham St Annes there were distinctions in the two communities which stirred powerful but well-meaning emotions.

With this in mind I hope you will understand why I see Lytham St Annes like a time machine. Lytham with its links back to the Doomsday book and St Annes with its origins in that great engine room of change the 19th century. Taken as a whole it represents one of the nicest parts of Lancashire and, indeed, the whole country and where the distinct character of each of the partners is there for all to see. Both are special and as this photographic record proves they have maintained their distinctiveness in a world which all too often seems hell bent on uniformity.

My congratulations go to those who have had the thoughtfulness to bring together these images in time for the benefit of this and future generations to enjoy and to celebrate.

MICHAEL JACK
MP FOR FYLDE

Lytham – The Grand Old Lady

LEAFY Lytham is without doubt the grand old lady of the Fylde Coast. With serene charm she is steeped in history and tradition, proud of her green finery in summer and of her heritage all the year round.

For countless centuries men have been winning a living from the sea and the land at the mouth of the River Ribble – and like all the best historical spots, Lytham was mentioned in the Doomsday book.

At one time it was the preserve of a man known as Ravenkill and in 1190 his grandson Richard gave Lytham to the Benedictine monks of Durham.

They established a priory in the lonely outpost and derived income from various sources which included ship's moorings, use of the common oven, grinding corn and the wrecks of the sea.

In 1606 Cuthbert Clifton of Westby bought the Manor of Lytham for £4,300 to begin a dynasty in the town which was to continue until 1963 when his descendant Harry de Vere Clifton sold out the last remnants of the family estate to Guardian Royal Assurance, for a great deal larger sum.

The Cliftons were to have a major influence on the development of the town but it was the Victorian boom in sea bathing that helped make Lytham what it is today.

Northern mill workers came in their droves to bathe, picnic and even drink the waters and Lytham benefited from being on the doorstep of Blackpool which was big, bold and unashamedly brassy.

Expansion was rapid from being a few fishermen's cottages, a market square and a handful of small hotels in the 1800s, the gentile seaside resort emerged.

The arrival of the railway in 1846 strengthened Lytham's singular appeal and as the bricks and concrete pushed back the farmland a love affair for many Northern families had truly begun and continues today.

The boom in sea bathing put Lytham on the map. By the mid-1850s the railway had arrived and the coastal village of farmers and fishermen was flourishing as a seaside resort. Generations of visitors loved nothing more than to walk along the picturesque Green to Lytham Windmill.

Long before the spread of spartina grass, families used to flock to the golden shores of Lytham, to what was dubbed a children's paradise.

Swingboats, ice cream kiosks and donkey rides were traditional attractions soon in place to satisfy the fascination of armies of day trippers who came, enjoyed and fell in love with the seaside.

A stroll out from the Lytham jetty to one of the sailing vessels at low tide. Such a walk would be extremely dangerous today because of the silt and mud.

During the summer hundreds of day trippers found their way to Lytham Pier, opened in 1865. Before the arrival of the railway they would travel by wagons, carts and light vehicles across the Freckleton Marsh toll road to go for an invigorating bathe in the sea or to picnic on the Green.

Lytham Pier in 1910 – there was no better vantage point to watch the busy River Ribble with sailing ships, pleasure craft and cargo vessels bound for Preston Docks. The pier fell into disrepair and despite a 2,593-residents petition in 1959 the town council refused to pay £5,000 to save it from the scrap merchants. It was demolished the following year.

In the 1890s a Pavilion was opened halfway down Lytham Pier and a Floral Hall was added at the seaward end to provide traditional seaside entertainment, including summer shows and band concerts. Here Miss Dorothea Vincent's Cremona Orchestra entertain.

Lytham Pier in its hey-day as visitors mill round the entrance kiosks covered in advertising hoardings and watch children's amusements on the beach.

The Pier after a storm in October 1903 when a pair of steel-hulled barges broke away from their moorings and crashed through the structure. The £1,400 repair bill was picked up by Preston Corporation after a court battle.

Aftermath of the 1928 blaze that destroyed the Lytham Pier Pavilion which at the time was in use as a cinema. The operating box can clearly be seen among the gutted ruins.   Ref No: LY1

Always a focal point of fascination, Lytham Windmill has been the town's most famous landmark for almost two centuries. Built around 1805 it was in use as a corn mill until the end of World War One. However, records show there were windmills in Lytham at the time of the Benedictine priory between 1190 and 1539, and a 17th-century map locates one near Lytham Hall.

On New Year's Day 1919 fire broke out which gutted the interior of the Mill and destroyed machinery inside. Since then it has seen numerous uses as a café, electricity sub station and headquarters for a motor boat club and Ribble Cruising Club. Today it has been fully restored by Fylde Borough Council as a tourist attraction.

14

The old lifeboat station alongside Lytham Windmill was built in 1844 by Colonel John Talbot Clifton, then Squire of Lytham, for just £298. Constructed largely of sea cobbles it is one of the oldest lifeboat houses on the coast. The first lifeboat was supplied by the Shipwrecked Fishermen's and Mariners' Society through local subscriptions. The building was taken over by the RNLI in 1854 and was in use until the new station opened in 1960. The old building then had a variety of owners before its present day and most fitting use as a permanent RNLI museum.

Crowds would turn out on the waters edge to watch the lifeboat being wheeled out of the station, lowered down the steep embankment and launched into the Ribble. Generations of Lytham fishermen have served on the lifeboat.

Away from the beach early Lytham comprised of little more than Clifton Street, Henry Street and the triangular piece of land occupied by the Market Hall, which stands on the site of the former village green and pinfold. The hall opened in 1848 and the clock tower was added in 1872. In the room above the Market Hall met the Board of Commissioners, predecessors of the Town Council.

The giant elm 'Old Tom', which stood between the County and the Market Building in Hastings Place until felled in 1981, is believed to be the original site of the village fish stones and stocks.

Bands regularly played in the Market Square which was originally occupied by a water fountain memorial erected by Lady Eleanor Cecily Clifton after the death of her husband in 1882. This Tucks card describes Lytham as 'an attractive Lancashire watering place, much quieter and therefore sought by a different type of tourists to the excursionists who fill Blackpool and Southport to overflowing.'

The former Clifton estate office, previously the site of the original gate to Lytham Hall. The Georgian-style office was built in the 1860s and it was here that Elijah Hargreaves came in 1874 to lease 600 acres of land from the Clifton family that were to signal the start of St Annes.   Ref No LY2

The tramway and approach to Lytham Pier from Dicconson Terrace, which was created in 1824 when the Wheatsheaf Hotel and adjoining buildings on the south side of Clifton Street were demolished.

Sign of the transport revolution. Passengers on board a gas tram which prepares to move from Dicconson Terrace into Church Road while the landau facing Park Street remains empty. The gas trams ran on coal gas pumped in at 16-mile intervals and travelled at 12mph. They were replaced by electrified trams in 1903.

Imposing glass verandah above Pearson's refreshment rooms and boarding establishment. Neighbouring Maypole Diary can also be seen in this 1905 picture of the corner of Clifton Square and Henry Street.

The white brick-built Palace cinema stands out among the shops in Clifton Street, Lytham. The cinema was built along with a café at a cost of £5,000 in 1930 but survived just 28 years before it was demolished. The site is now occupied by Arndale House and includes F.W.Woolworth and Boots.

Open top trams stopped in Clifton Street near the Ship Hotel while a landau hurries through from Dicconson Terrace bound for Park Street, passing the sunken public conveniences in the foreground.

A lone tram travels along the single track at what today is one of the busiest junctions in the town. The Market Hall and water fountain can be seen in the background as well as the former Clifton Estate Office. J.W.Stringer (right), one of Lytham's oldest businesses, occupies its prime corner site as it does today. The original company was founded in 1857 by Ferdinand Naples. The name changed to Stringers in 1898.

Banners, flags and bunting in Lytham Square in 1935 – not for Club Day but for the Silver Jubilee of King George V and Queen Mary. The first screening at the Palace Theatre (left) was *Gold Diggers of Broadway* on 21 April 1930. Mrs Violet Clifton travelled specially from her home Kildalton Castle on the Isle of Islay for the opening ceremony.   Ref No: LY3

All forms of transport in this busy town centre scene outside the Ship Hotel in Clifton Street as tram, car, horse and bicycle take to the road. Trams trundled along Clifton Street between 1896 and 1936. The Ship is believed to be haunted by the ghost of a tall dark stranger said to be Squire John Talbot Clifton.

The trams have gone and the age of the double-decker bus has arrived, not to mention cars and vans in busy Clifton Street, a far cry from the early days of white thatched cottages of mud and cobble. The buses took over from the trams in 1936.

A near deserted Park Street with walled residential properties on the south side of the road. Under the glass verandah (left) is the E.H.Booth store, which has since moved to Market Square, and further along almost hidden from view is the Wesleyan Chapel.

The Roman Corinthian columns of the Wesleyan Chapel in Park Street which is today the Methodist Chapel. It was built in 1868 to replace a smaller chapel in Bath Street, now a clinic, erected in 1847 thanks to the generosity of Thomas Crouch Hincksman.

Horse traffic only on Westby Street, a terrace of smart new terraced properties in the expanding town.

Many middle-class families moved to Lytham and found the well-built terraced properties in Cecil Street, like those in Westby Street, to their liking, ideally situated for the town centre.

Horses and trams share Church Road, one of the main thoroughfares between Lytham and St Annes and eventually Blackpool. The centre section of the road was laid in setts by the tram company while the outside was tarmacadamed by the council.

The County and Commercial Hotel was one of the four principal hotels in the early days of Lytham. It was built in the early 1800s and was originally called the Market Hotel.

The Clifton Arms Hotel showing a fenced garden frontage. The original hotel stood on the north side of Clifton Street, across what is now the entrance to Park Street. It was demolished in 1839 and rebuilt on its present site, dominating the Green.

Charlie's Mast is one of Lytham's historic landmarks. The 60-foot flagpole has stood proudly opposite the Clifton Arms Hotel for more than a century. The mast had been a navigation aid for Ribble shipping and owes its name to Charlie Townsend, an old guinea trader who set up a lantern on a cart shaft to signal passing vessels bound for Lytham's mud dock before Preston Dock existed. Lytham Improvement Commissioners eventually took over the responsibility for the mast's upkeep.

More evidence of the popularity of Lytham Promenade. This is a 1913 view of the packed pathway as visitors choose to sit, stroll or look out across the Ribble estuary.

Lytham Green was constructed in the late 18th century to protect the town from flooding after 40 houses were swept away in December 1720. The levelling began at the east end of the 'Marsh' as it was then called. It was handed over to the town by the Clifton family in 1923.

Fine well-built houses began to spring up on the fashionable seafront as the resort rapidly grew. The White Cottage was one of a handful of original properties on the front, and is believed to have been used as a hunting lodge by the Cliftons.

Looking west on Lytham Promenade. The long since gone sandy beach with donkeys, swing boats and amusements, in the background alongside Lytham Pier, attracted the crowds.

Even the very young got the chance to ride on a donkey on Lytham Green as this 1915 view clearly proves. It is hard to believe that the green was once an area of sand dunes. Stone was brought from Cumbria to create the sea wall. Happily a 1950s bid to drive a dual carriageway through the Green failed.

Just as busy as ever in the 1950s, this paddling pool and sand pit known as Lytham Lido, was a children's paradise, especially as the state of the beach steadily declined.   Ref No: LY4

A more sombre occasion on Lytham Green as Lord Derby prepares to inspect the troops during World War One. Some 4,000 raw recruits trained in Lytham and St Annes.

Lytham Swimming Baths. The original shareholders were Charles and Ceswald Lister Swainson, James Eden and Thomas Fair who were paid off when the property came under the ownership of the Squire in 1886.

Lytham Baths where generations of Lytham and St Annes children first learned to swim. The building also included a concert hall and ballroom but sadly became dilapidated under council ownership and was closed in 1987. The Assembly Rooms have since been given a new lease of life, administered by a Town Trust, and now comprise of a modern community rooms, a revamped Lytham Yacht Club headquarters and seafront flats.

Ref No: LY5

The impressive façade of the Lytham Baths building, originally built in 1862 but extended to this neo-Georgian style in 1927.

Ref No: LY6

Swimmers waiting for another plunge from the Lytham Baths diving boards, pictured in January 1953. Lytham Urban District Council took over the maintenance of baths from the Clifton family in 1920. Ref LY7

Lytham saw the birth of ships which sailed the world. At its peak the Lytham Shipbuilding and Engineering Company employed 400 men in the Creek shipyard. During World War One the yard worked night and day building ships for the Admiralty. Pictured is the twin-screw passenger and cargo ship *Fantiman*. The last vessel built at the yard in 1954 was the Windermere ferry *Drake*. The yard went into liquidation in 1955 as the silting of the Ribble took its toll.

Lytham's fishing industry continued to flourish through the 1950s and into the 1960s. Here mussels just arrived from Morecambe are unloaded at the Lytham purification works in 1945. The tanks were widely regarded as an eyesore on Lytham's beauty. They later became the sailing dinghy pens at Ribble Cruising Club.

Ref No: LY8

Bath Street was so called because bathing vans operated from among the many boarding houses. There are many fine houses on the terraced street, fronted by intricate pebble patterned pavements, dated 1831 and 1848. In the 1950s they were in danger of being lost under a layer of asphalt until the influential Mrs Violet Clifton intervened. The vans were introduced in 1820 by builder Thomas Miller who not only ran people out to the sea to bathe but touted the village in search of customers. On wet Sundays the same vans were also used by Lytham's large churchgoing population.

Ref No: LY9

The Queens Hotel on the corner of Bath Street and Central Beach was built in 1854 and was originally called The Neptune.

St Cuthbert's Parish Church, erected in 1834. It is the third church of the name to serve the parish since its foundation in the 12th century and cost £1,600. It was actually built around the older church so services could continue without interruption.

St Cuthbert's vicarage, which stands hidden away on Church Road. The rectory is believed to have been originally built by the Squire of Lytham for his horse trainer.

Ref No: LY10

For 100 years these bells called people to worship at St Cuthbert's Parish Church. However, they remained silent for three months in 1947 when they were returned and recast at a foundry in Whitechapel, London.   Ref No: LY11

Lytham's memorial to the men who perished in the *Mexico* lifeboat disaster in 1886 stands at the rear of St Cuthbert's churchyard.   Ref No: LY12

An unusual postcard view of St Cuthbert's Parish Church, as seen from the graveyard behind the church.

St Cuthbert's Cross, hidden among the hedgerow on Church Road. According to tradition the body of St Cuthbert rested here about the year 882 on the way to Durham Cathedral.

Ref No: LY13

A Lytham landmark demolished in 1960 was the Customs House at the east of Lytham Green which made way for the Land Registry offices. It was occupied in the 1850s by principal customs officer Mr Thomas Cookson, whose duties were to check for smuggling and collect harbour dues. The Customs House was used to store contraband and also as a mortuary for bodies washed up on the beach. When new offices opened at Preston Dock the house fell into decay but was later used as an art studio and headquarters by Lytham Sea Cadets.   Ref No: LY14

Lytham Cottage Hospital and Convalescent Home, built in 1871 by the Squire of Lytham, Colonel John Talbot Clifton, who donated it to the town. Like many of Lytham's older buildings it was constructed of brick and sea cobbles. This photograph was taken in 1928 after modernisation work to the wing.   Ref No: LY15

Among the fine properties built as Lytham prospered was the private school Lowther College, named as Lowther Gardens and Lowther Terrace to commemorate the family name of Lady Eleanor Cecily Clifton, who made many generous gifts to the town.

The Home of Rest, one of a growing number of large convalescent homes which sprang up as the elderly recognised the benefits of salt-sea air and water, and moved to the coast.

The Westwood Miners Home was built at the turn of the century but proved too costly to run for the Miners Welfare Society who sold up in 1981. The demolition of the magnificent property which looked out over Lytham Cricket Club, provoked angry reaction as many bidders wanted to preserve it as a children's home, even a hotel and restaurant. Today the site is occupied by Westwood Mews in Church Road. Ref No: LY16

The life's work of the late Archdeacon H.L.Fosbrooke, vicar of Lytham until 1944, was the care of retired clergymen. This 1952 photograph is of the conservatory of Fosbrooke House on Clifton Drive, Lytham. It was named after him and was the first home of its kind in the north.   Ref No: LY17

Sandbags piled high as war preparations are made in 1939 outside the police station and magistrates courts in Bannister Street, which were built in an Edwardian baroque style with a red-brick tower and wrought iron balcony.

Ref No: LY18

The wartime generosity of Lytham St Annes is seen here in the presentation of a vehicle for the St John Ambulance Association presented by the Lytham and Ansdell voluntary aid detachment.

Crash site of a Junkers 88 German bomber which was shot down in flames by a Defiant on 4 April 1941. Wreckage was strewn across the River Ribble banks off Lytham. Six months later the town suffered its biggest wartime tragedy when one person was killed and another five injured by a bomb dropped on a house in Church Road, St Annes.   Ref No: LY19

VE Day street parties to celebrate the end of World War Two were held throughout Lytham. Pictured are the 1945 festivities in the aptly named Victoria Street.

St Peter's RC Church at the corner of Clifton Street and Station Road was built in 1839. Previously Roman Catholics had worshipped in a small chapel belonging to Lytham Hall. Station Road took its name because the first railway station stood on the site of the existing fire station.

St John's Parish Church, overlooking Lytham Green and the Windmill, was erected in 1849 on land given by the Clifton family. Lifeboat services are held each year at St John's which became a separate parish in 1870.

The old St John's vicarage, which like many of Lytham's oldest properties was constructed in both brick and sea cobbles, was demolished in October 1967. The original St John's School was built in 1851 but was demolished in 1987 to make way for sheltered housing.　　Ref No: LY20

Lytham Congregational Church, today known as Lytham United Reformed Church, was built at the corner of Bannister Street and Westby Street in 1852.

One of the most distinctive of Clifton Street town house properties is Mulberry House, opposite the Lytham Library and Institute.

The imposing Lytham Institute building on the corner of Clifton Street and Bannister Street, built in 1878, and still a cornerstone of community life – in use as the public library.
Ref No: LY21

Leafy Lytham was an inescapable image of the developing town, even in quieter spots such as Mythop Avenue, pictured here in 1952.   Ref No: LY22

Tree-lined Green Drive has been a favourite woodland walk for decades. The beauty spot was given by the Squire of Lytham, John Talbot Clifton to celebrate the Golden Jubilee of the founding of St Annes in 1875.

Ballam Road, sometimes referred on post-cards as Invalid's walk, bordering the Lytham Hall estate has always presented the town's leafy image, which was further strengthened by a great tree planting programme started by the Cliftons in the 1850s.

There must have been quite a light and quite a celebration at this grand daddy of all bonfires, built on Lytham foreshore to celebrate the Coronation of George V in 1911. Lytham Pier Pavilion stands in the distance.

Despite the march of seaside progress, Lytham has maintained a strong farming tradition on its rich arable land. Here Mr William Harrison (driving) and his brother Roger harvest oats at Moss Side Hall Farm, Moss Side, Lytham, in August 1951. They were the fourth generation of their family to farm the land. Ref No: LY23

To this day small fishing boats have remained a common sight on the banks of the Ribble at Lytham, although the shell fishing industry has sadly declined.
Ref No: LY24

Lowther Gardens, entered through impressive wrought iron gates, were given to the town by the Cliftons in 1905. In the 1870s the area was an expanse of common land known as 'Hungry Moor'.

Squire of Lytham John Talbot Clifton laid out the gardens in 1873 and named them after his wife Lady Eleanor Cecily Clifton whose family name was Lowther.

Lowther Pavilion, has been the backbone of the local community amateur dramatic and entertainment scene, particularly after fire destroyed the Ashton Theatre in St Annes in 1977.

The peaceful Lowther gardens have remained one of the main attractions of the resort for generations of holidaymakers and residents alike.

Lytham Hall – ancestral home of the Clifton family, Squires of Lytham, who played an influential role in the development of both Lytham and St Annes. The original manor was bought by Cuthbert Clifton in 1906. The present day Georgian frontage was designed by eminent architect John Carr of York and was completed in 1764.

Swiss Lodge which stands at the entrance to Green Drive was once part of the Clifton family estate. It was built in 1884 in memory of Thomas Henry Clifton MP who died four years earlier at the age of 35.

Church Road Lodge made of traditional brick and sea cobbles, which are also to be seen in the wall and the imposing gateway pillars. The cobbled wall originally stretched along the entire boundary of the Clifton estate, and can still be seen today.

Watch Wood Lodge on Ballam Road was another of the entrances to Lytham Hall which would be maintained by a lodge keeper at the turn of the century.

The imposing main entrance gates to the Lytham Hall are thought to have originally stood not far from the Lytham Estates Office in Hastings Place. They were moved in anticipation of the arrival of the railway.

Squire of Lytham Mr John Talbot Clifton (far left) whose best remembered gifts to the town were Lowther Gardens and Lytham Green Drive. He is pictured at the Grand Hotel, St Annes in March 1925 with his family before receiving the freedom of Lytham St Annes. The other members of the family are (from left): Miss Easter Clifton, Mrs Violet Clifton, Michael Clifton and eldest son and heir Talbot de Vere Clifton. The Squire died in the Canary Islands in March 1928.

Ref No: LY25

On a visit to Lytham Hall in 1955, Mrs Violet Clifton, aged 71 and her youngest son Michael. She returned to spend her last days at the hall after leaving a convent in the South of England. Mrs Clifton died in 1961 and is buried in Lytham St Annes Park Cemetery.

Ref No: LY26.

Harry Clifton pictured in 1938. Members of the Clifton family were stunned when they read Evelyn Waugh's *Brideshead Revisited*, part of which was written when he stayed with Harry, an Oxford contemporary at Lytham Hall three years earlier.

The family believed that Waugh had, in part based some of his characters on their family. In letters written from Lytham Hall in 1935 Waugh said it was a house 'in the lap of luxury flowing with champagne and elaborate cookery.' He described the Clifton children as 'bright and giggling' and the Squire's mother Mrs Violet Clifton as being 'more sombre and full of soul'.

Ref No: LY29

Lilian Clifton, Harry's glamorous American-born actress wife. A divorcee from a wealthy Bostonian family she married him two weeks after they met but the whirlwind high society marriage was not to last.   Ref LY28

The colourful former Squire of Lytham Mr Harry Clifton pictured on his return to Lytham Hall in October 1962. Four years later he was to sell off the last of his family's land – and the Hall – to Guardian. Mr Clifton spent much of his later life living on the French Riviera and usually stayed at the Ritz in London when back in this country. He died in 1979.   Ref No: LY27

The hanging of an oil painting of the first president of Lytham Conservative Club, Mr John Talbot Clifton in March 1927. Pictured with the painting is club vice-president Mr Humphrey Whittle (left) and president Mr James Ashton.

Ref No: LY30

The memorial fountain erected in Market Square by Lady Eleanor Cecily Clifton in memory of her husband who died in 1882. The fountain was later moved to its present peaceful site in Sparrow Park, off Station Square.

Ref No: LY31

Lytham Cenotaph was unveiled on 14 January 1922 in the gardens of the Market Square, the Clifton memorial fountain having been moved to Sparrow Park.

The formal opening of Queen Mary School, Lytham, by Lord Derby in November 1930. It was built at a cost of £75,000 from the funds of the Lytham Schools Foundation which also provided the King Edward VII School in 1909. Queen Mary started the school year with 154 girls but by the end of the year this had risen to 268.
Ref No: LY32.

Miss Doris Bailey the first headmistress of Queen Mary School, plants a tree to commemorate King George VI's Coronation in 1937. Each girl received a medal and book to mark the event. Miss Bailey retired in 1952 and died in Harrogate in 1971.   Ref No: LY33

King Edward VII School, Lytham, owes its birth to the Rev W.Threlfall, vicar of Lytham who in 1702 gave £5 to a fund to provide a school. The fund grew into the Lytham School Charities Foundation, following shrewd investment in Blackpool land. Headroomgate Road was one of two sites considered for the school but it was finally decided in 1904 to buy 32 acres from the Clifton family and Fairhaven Estate Company for £22,000. The school opened in September 1908. The first headmaster was Mr H.Bompas Smith who was selected from 185 applicants.   Ref No: LY34

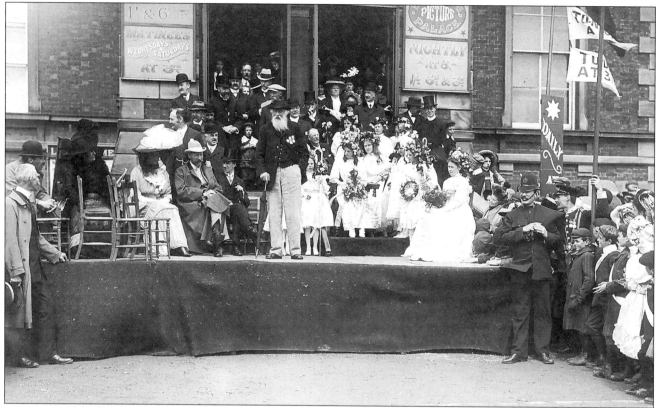

No pictorial look at Lytham's past would be complete without mention of Lytham Club Day which has been part of the character and fabric of the developing town. The parade of clubs and societies was already more than half a century old when the first rose queen was crowned in 1894. The earliest ceremonies were conducted outside the Lytham Baths before the event grew so large that the festivities were transferred to Lowther Gardens. The central figure is Wykeham Clifton of Warton Hall.

The crowning ceremony of Mary Clacoe in Lowther Gardens in 1909. Wykeham Clifton could eventually proudly boast that he had crowned more than 20 queens.

A sea of young faces, most of them in fancy dress, enjoy a rendition by a quartet of Tartan entertainers on the Lowther Gardens stage.

Crowds line the route of the Club Day procession, just as they do today.

Scouts provide a guard of honour for a landau carrying one of the church rose queens.

The heavy wear and tear on this farm cart seems to have been well hidden by plenty of foliage for the procession of Grecian girls from St John's Sunday School in the 1905 Club Day procession.

A queen in all her glory accompanied by her attendants in a landau decorated in flowers for Lytham's great day of the year.

The Mayoress of Lytham St Annes, Mrs J.A.Hinchcliffe crowns Miss Jean Fielden the Lytham diamond jubilee rose queen in 1954.

Ref No: LY35

Ansdell and Fairhaven – The Spread of Suburbia

The sedate suburbs of Ansdell and Fairhaven expanded to fill the wasteland between Lytham and St Annes, bringing the two communities closer together. Amalgamation eventually came in 1922.

The sturdy white-walled, thatched cottages of Commonside, Ansdell, are believed to have been built with timbers from vessels shipwrecked in the Ribble. Their walls were described as being 'clumped, stood, raddled and daubed'. This meant the clay was shaped into bricks (clumped). The bricks were then placed in position (stood) were cleaned off (raddled) and finally daubed in whitewash – which was even used on the sea cobble garden walls.

Commonside contained some of the oldest thatched cottages in Lytham St Annes until the late 1940s when many were demolished to make way for road improvements.

Smart town house properties in Rossall Road, Ansdell, described by their datestones as villas and built in 1897. The growing community took its name from Richard Ansdell, a famous 19th-century painter of sporting and outdoor scenes, who built a large house and studio named Starr Hills, looking out over the Ribble.

The cottages were home to fishermen, farmers and also workmen employed on the Clifton estate lands. Pictured right is a quaint cottage, which is still to be seen, with its prominent dormer and slate-roofed porch, which was a traditional Fylde feature.

Ivy-covered Commonside Farm in Ansdell was built in the mid-1800s among the earlier fishermen's thatched cottages. This 1908 view clearly shows the rugged road which existed with no footpath (left).

Before World War One new properties of traditional bricks and mortar began to spring up in Gordon Road in contrast to the white-walled cottages on the opposite side of the road.

Not a motor car in sight in this 1920s view of Woodlands Road, looking down the bridge towards the Ansdell Institute and public hall built in 1909 (left) with St Joseph's RC Church in the distance.

The growth of Ansdell can clearly be seen in this view of Milner Road, looking across the railway and Oxford Road.

Oxford Road, Ansdell in 1914. The fence on the right runs along the side of the railway line and Skew Bridge is just visible in the distance.

Many a holiday was spent at the Rossendale boarding house at the corner of Woodlands Road and Clifton Drive. The mock Tudor building has retained its name and today is known as the New Rossendale Nursing Home.

Two churches together – the Wesleyan Church, better known as Fairhaven Methodist Church built at the corner of Woodlands Road and Clifton Drive towers over the earlier Methodist Mission.

Clifton Drive, Ansdell in 1907 – with the Rossendale boarding house in the distance but the Fairhaven Methodist Church had not yet been built.

Lytham College in splendid isolation on the landward side of Clifton Drive, near to Woodlands Road. It was a boys' boarding and day school with the luxury of its own tennis court alongside. The property has been converted into flats – although one of the entrances is still clearly marked 'Boys'.

Worshippers must have found facilities fairly basic at the original Ansdell Baptist Church in 1905 which was replaced by the existing red-brick built church in Ansdell Road North in 1908.

Many a happy holiday was spent on the sands at Children's corner in Granny's Bay, Fairhaven. Until 1885 the bay was also used by the fishermen of Lytham, Heyhouses and Commonside for anchorage in rough weather. A bid to build beach chalets in the bay was refused in 1958.

Starr Hills was the home of Richard Ansdell between 1860 and 1872. The house was used as a Red Cross centre in both world wars and for the past 40 years has been a Methodist Homes for the Aged. A grand-daughter of a former owner of Starr Hills, Major William Henry Hincksman, Dr Dorothy Hincksman Farrar, vice-president of the Methodist conference, was one of the VIP guests at the official opening in June 1958.

Ref No:LY36

An early photograph of St Paul's Church, Ansdell, when the footpaths of Clifton Drive were still unsurfaced and Lake Road (far left) which also appears unmade.

Ref No: LY37

Two adjoining houses in unmade St Paul's Avenue were used as the clubhouse of Fairhaven Golf Club until it moved to its present Hall Park site in 1921. The club was founded in 1895 and the course originally spanned both sides of Clifton Drive near Queen Mary School. The first clubhouse is now Fairhaven Lake café.

Fairhaven Hotel, built in September 1895, loomed large over Granny's Bay until it was demolished in January 1976, to be replaced by the present Boddingtons pub.   Ref No: LY38

One of the most recognisable landmarks on the Fairhaven skyline remains the White Church. The magnificent Byzantine building built of white-glazed brick was founded in 1904 and can be seen from miles around.

Granny's Bay after tidal floods in October 1931 appear to have created a second Fairhaven Lake. The lake was born in the same manner – tidal water being caught between two River banks of sand, shingle and cobbles.   Ref No: LY39

A 1916 view of the Inner Promenade at Fairhaven showing the densely covered lake embankment, long before the addition of any corner shelters and public toilets. There was also plenty of prime building on the Promenade, ripe for development.

Fairhaven Lake was one of the gifts given to the town by generous benefactor Lord Ashton. He gave £34,000 to buy the lake, sometimes known as Ashton Marine Park, in 1926.

There was no shortage of youngsters wanting to trip around the lake in 1935. Note also the gardens on the embankment by the brick-built Lake entrance and the overlooking Promenade mansions.   Ref No: LY40

Stepping stones through one of the smaller Marine Park lakes at Fairhaven, which was later filled in and landscaped.

Crowds regularly flocked to Fairhaven to see exciting water sports such as hydroplane racing in August 1955. Ref No: LY41

Thrills and spills of a water-skiing spectacular at Fairhaven Lake in the 1950s.

Ref No: LY42

ST-ANNES-ON-THE-SEA

St Annes – The Brash Newcomer from the Sandhills

ST ANNES is testimony to the foresight and spirit of the seaside pioneers.

In 1800 there was little to St Annes – or Lytham's West End as it was then known – beyond a few farm and fishing cottages among the vast wilderness of sandhills.

All that started to change when cotton magnate Elijah Hargreaves from the Rossendale Valley, holidaying in Blackpool, wandered south along the beach and visualised a new town.

In 1874 he and seven fellow directors registered the St Annes Land and Building Company and the romantic birth of a new resort had begun.

The town, of course, took its name from the church of St Anne, given in 1873 by Lady Eleanor Cecily Clifton of Lytham.

The first property was the St Annes Hotel and the Squire of Lytham, Mr John Talbot Clifton, then seven years of age, laid the foundation of the new town which grew at a rapid pace.

The pioneers vision was of a garden city, on the doorstep of booming Blackpool but determined to stamp its own identity on the Fylde Coast pleasure ground.

The company didn't take long to decide to build a pier as they felt that the sea at St Annes afforded better boating and fishing than could be had at any sea port on the West coast. The baths, boating pool, lake and golf courses followed to form a smart, sophisticated holiday town which soon earned the title The Opal of the West.

The resort attracted holiday hordes, private schools and also retired people seeking a peaceful and healthy retreat after the stresses of business life.

And as the hotels and boarding houses, convalescent and nursing homes

sprang up, so did the stately mansions of wealthy businessmen who made their homes by the sea while travelling each day into the grimy hinterland of industrial Lancashire.

For many years St Annes flirted seriously with the idea of amalgamating with Blackpool, but the idea was dropped in favour of the merger of Lytham and St Annes in May 1922.

Today its name is known throughout Britain as the headquarters of both the Football League and ERNIE the Premium Bond computer, and worldwide as one of the outstanding venues of the prestigious British Open Golf Championship.

The wilderness that was St Annes in 1880. Sand dunes, spartina grass and rabbit warrens abounded on windswept undeveloped land occupied by farmers and fishermen. Pictured centre is St Annes Parish Church built in 1873.

Ref No: SA1

Elijah Hargreaves, the cotton magnate from the Rossendale Valley and founder of St Annes, who first had a vision of the garden city.

South Promenade before its many improvements that were to transform the resort into the 'Opal of the West'. In the distance stood the Old Lighthouse which was situated opposite what is now aptly named Lightburne Avenue.

The first Sandgrown'uns lived off the land and the sea. Women folk spent many back-breaking hours raking up cockles off the beach.

St Annes Pier has been the town's central seaside attraction for more than 100 years. Hundreds of people crammed the pier to witness the official opening on 15 June 1885, by Lord Derby, Col. Fred Stanley MP. Generations have since been drawn to stroll along its wooden decking.

The pier was originally 315 yards long with a 40-foot jetty that reached out into the channel. It was used by fishing vessels and a variety of sailing craft and pleasure boats – including steamers who ran regular trips along the coast, to Lytham, Southport, Liverpool, Morecambe and Fleetwood.

Like a frontier of the old west, St Annes rapidly took shape. It is hard to believe this was North Crescent looking inland towards St Annes Road East in 1885. The property on the right in St David's Road South is now occupied by shops. A start on work on the Our Lady Star of the Sea Church was not made for a further three years.

The timber lighthouse which stood on the dunes at what is now the corner of Lightburne Avenue and South Promenade. The lighthouse was erected in 1865 following the collapse of its stone-predecessor two years earlier. It became a well-known landmark, popular with picnic parties from Blackpool.

St Annes Hotel was the first of the new buildings in St Annes, its first turf being cut in February 1875. Squire John Talbot Clifton was only seven years old when the following month he laid the foundation stone which launched the new town.

Among the first homes in St Annes were Clifton Cottages in Church Road, then known as Common Lane. The properties were originally thatched.

Ref No: SA2

One of the earliest photographs of the lifeboat monument, unveiled in May 1888 following the *Mexico* lifeboat disaster in December 1886 when 13 heroic members of the St Annes lifeboat *Laura Janet* and 14 crew of the Southport lifeboat lost their lives trying to save the crew of the *Mexico* which ran aground in the Ribble estuary.   Ref No: SA3

St Annes Promenade in the 1890s. The Promenade Gardens were beginning to take shape but there was no boating pool, no iron sandshield Promenade wall and no open air baths.   Ref No: SA4

Newly-built St Annes Parish Church. Lady Eleanor Cecily Clifton provided the money for the building of the chapel of ease with a small spire which opened in 1873 to serve the isolated West End farmers and fishermen.
Ref No: SA5

An early seafront landmark was The Bungalow, built in 1890s for local historian and solicitor Mr H.T.Croft, which was one of the most modern designs of its day. With its commanding views of the coastline it was bought by the great Victorian benefactor and golf baron Lord Ashton, who loved the resort, and was one of the main figures in its rapid development. The property was demolished in the 1960s and the site today is occupied by houses in Cartmell Road and on the Inner Promenade.
Ref No: SA6

The town's fire service was formed in 1888 when the bell from a past shipwreck would be sounded from near the police station. Firemen had to pull a handcart pump until a horse-drawn engine was introduced. Volunteers are pictured outside the fire station in 1908. A red-brick house and engine hall was built in 1920 in St Andrews Road North, St Annes, and was later replaced in 1985.   Ref No: SA7

North Promenade with its typical William Porritt properties of East Lancashire stone and yellow brick which are the Edwardian character of the central square mile of St Annes.

William Porritt, the wealthy Lancashire cotton merchant, who helped give St Annes its distinctively elegant image by investing some £250,000 in building new property in the town – a sizeable fortune in the 1890s.

St Annes begins to consolidate as a residential area as shown in this view of York Road but it must have still been a bumpy ride for a horse and cart as the road was as yet unmade.
Ref No: SA8

This 1905 view of Derby Road was typical of the developing new town. It clearly shows the concept of wide streets on which the Victorian new resort was based – a far cry from the back-to-back terraces of the mill towns where many of St Annes early citizens had made their money.   Ref No: SA9

One of the earliest properties on St Annes seafront was the Ormerod Home opened in 1890 by Lady Eleanor Cecily Clifton. Over the years thousands of children spent some time here sent from the industrial towns to convalesce in the bracing sea air. The old Ormerod was eventually bulldozed to make way for a luxury housing development but its name lives on as a Trust in North Promenade, St Annes.

The Grand Hotel was one of the first hotels in St Annes, built in 1897 by the Holloway family and catering for well-to-do Victorian families. It was eventually sold in May 1950 to meet the heavy duties and taxes on the will of Miss Kitty Holloway who had managed the hotel after her parent's death.

One of the finest examples of St Annes architecture was the Clifton Private Hotel on the corner of Hornby Road and the Promenade, with its large gables, impressive bow windows and elaborate balconies and walled gardens. Sadly it was demolished soon after World War Two.

St Annes Golden Jubilee Year 1925 began with the purchase of the Southdown Hydro opposite St Annes Pier which became, and still is today, the Town Hall.

On the opposite corner of the Promenade and St Annes Road East stood St Annes largest hotel, the Majestic, originally known as the Imperial Hydro, which was completed in 1910. The central bronze statue often thought to have been Bodicea was, in fact, Hygeia – the goddess of health. It was melted down for munitions during World War Two.

With 200 bedrooms, a swimming pool and tennis courts the Majestic earned a reputation as the height of luxury.

It was a sad day in 1975 when the Majestic hotel was demolished to make way for a five-storey development of new luxury apartments. Famous guests at the Majestic had included Winston Churchill, Danny Kaye, Margaret Lockwood, the Marx Brothers, Tyrone Power and Kim Novak.
Ref No: SA10

At the turn of the century numerous small independent schools sprang up in the new garden city of St Annes. One of the earliest was Kilgrimol School in Clifton Drive South, opened for boarding and day school boys in 1875. The building is still recognisable today and remains an all-male establishment – the St Annes District Club.

Physical drill at Kilgrimol School. The boys used a large undeveloped area of St Thomas Road between the Royal Lytham Golf Club and Church Road as their playing fields.

Lawrence House did not falter like many of the early independent schools. It opened in 1906 as a preparatory school for boys overlooking Royal Lytham. The first Headmaster Mr C.D.G.Hoare had just 23 pupils. This building had a dual use as woodwork classroom and gymnasium.

The rifle range of Lawrence House. The school closed in 1993 when merger plans fell through. The following year it was bulldozed to make way for a luxury housing development.

Sandy Knoll was another of the numerous private schools which grew up. When firemen tackled a fire in the schoolroom in 1891 principal John Thompson was so grateful he invited all the firemen back the following night for supper.

The gym at Sandy Knoll School. Both these cards were posted in 1912 by boarder Edward Sergeant and were sent to his parents in Wrea Green. Sergeant later became Squire of Kirkham.

St Annes College for Girls was originally founded in around 1882 by two sisters Francis and Lilly Oldfield who came to the resort six years later and built a new school complete with tennis courts. Only one of the tall imposing 19th-century properties still remains, the other building and courts were sold in the 1960s. In the 1930s when this photograph was taken, the College had amalgamated, to become the St Annes and Saxonholme College.   Ref No: SA11

St Annes Technical College opened in 1907 alongside the St Annes Carnegie Library. It is now part of the Blackpool and Fylde College campus.

The tram line was originally opened from Squires Gate to St Annes, to be followed a year later by an extension to Lytham. By 1903 there was an electrified double line, seen here as it cuts through the sandhills on Clifton Drive North.

Three trams trundle along Clifton Drive South in 1915, passing the King's Road Methodist Church which has since been demolished. Also pictured (right) is St Annes Library, opened in January 1906, a gift to the town by benefactor Andrew Carnegie.

A tram heads towards St Annes Square along Clifton Drive North in the days before the prime corner site was developed. Trees abound where today stands St Annes Conservative Club and the Woolworth Buildings. The distinctive tram waiting room is still in use today as a tourist information office.

Charabancs arrive and depart at St Annes railway station in the days before motor taxis. The station had to wait until 1925 to be considerably enlarged and improved, by then the town's population had risen from a few hundred in 1880 to 15,000.

Ref No: SA12

Tickets please! A proud porter standing in front of advertising hoardings on the St Annes railway station platform in the 1920s. The first railway station master was a Mr Cookson who held the post for 20 years. He was succeeded by a Mr Parr who retired in 1923 after 25 years.

The age of steam as a locomotive heads north out of St Annes railway station towards Blackpool's South Shore. Grass fires were a common occurrence in the summer as embers flew on to the embankments. The line has since been reduced to a single-track shuttle service between South Shore and Kirkham.

The Empire picture house in St George's Road, St Annes, built in 1912, later to become the Plaza Cinema and then Studios 123. Today it remains an important attraction as the Plaza Entertainment Centre incorporating Clifton Casino and Plaza Bingo Club.

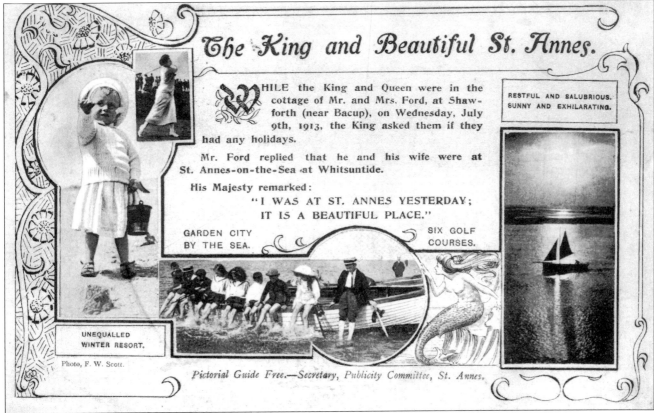

A resort fit for a king. For in July 1913 the town received royal recognition from King George V, who travelled slowly through the Fylde by car accompanied by Queen Mary *en route* to Blackpool. Schoolchildren lined the Promenade outside St Annes Pier and a band played to the large crowds. ``It is a beautiful place,'' King George said several days later on a visit to Shawforth, near Bacup and his words were transposed on to a postcard to last the test of time.

Healthy sea air and water encouraged guests to stay at establishments such as the Dunes House Hydro on the corner of Fairhaven Road and Clifton Drive South. It later became the Bradford District Rechabites Memorial Home, but a distinctive Dunes House 1898 datestone can still be seen.

Parasols head for the prom. Not a vehicle in sight in this view of St Annes Road West looking from the Pier forecourt towards the Square.

St Ives Hotel in the 1890s bears no resemblance to the sprawling seafront hotel complex it is today. Like the neighbouring Fernlea and Dalmeny, the hotels began life as little more than boarding houses but rapidly expanded and extended to become year-round family holiday centres, and the backbone of the St Annes tourist trade.

A far cry from today – the absence of traffic makes St Andrews Road South look an attractive tree-lined thoroughfare in 1919.

Hard to imagine that at the turn of the century this was Wood Street, St Annes. The trees, walls and private gardens have long since disappeared to make way for shops, offices and forecourt parking.

The well-heeled residents of St Annes had mansions with gardens grounds to match which meant boom time business for the nurserymen and landscape gardeners in the area such as Benjamin Singleton – the author's great-grandfather – who a had a large work force, an office in St Patrick's Road South and a nursery in Heyhouses Lane in the 1920s.

A wild, undeveloped corner of St Annes Road East and Carlton Road in 1905 with the Crescent and St Annes Pier entrance just visible in the background.

Boarding houses in St Albans Road, St Annes, provided more reasonably priced holiday accommodation for middle-class families who made the annual pilgrimage from inland industrial towns to Lytham St Annes – and big brother Blackpool.

Imposing buildings with wrought iron fenced walls, summer house and flagpole at the corner of Park Road and Wood Street, St Annes, now best known as Margaret's florists.

An age of elegance. Well-heeled members of St Annes Lawn Tennis Club on the opening day of the 1929 season.

An unusual view of Our Lady Star of the Sea Church at the bottom of the Crescent and corner of St Annes Road East. The foundation stone was laid in October 1888 and the church opened in June 1890. Members of the Clifton family and the Duke of Norfolk were among those present.

The Football League headquarters opened in July 1960. Thousands of pounds were spent on converting the former Sandown Hotel in Clifton Drive South after the move from Starkie Street, Preston, where the Football League had been based since it was formed in 1888.   Ref No: SA13

The Wesleyan Chapel built in 1892 known today as the Drive Methodist Church. It stands on the corner of East Bank Road alongside the old lifeboat, which was in operation between 1879 and 1925.

St Annes second lifeboat the *Nora Royds* outside the Lifeboat House. Wealthy businessman Charles Macara of North Promenade, pictured next to the wheel, organised the first Lifeboat Day street collection in Manchester. He lost many personal friends in the *Mexico* disaster and went on to organise a national appeal to help the 16 widows and 50 orphans left by the tragedy.

Launching the lifeboat at St Annes meant the need for horses and plenty of volunteers as the craft had to be pulled along East Bank Road from the station across the Promenade and down a stone slaid to the beach.

THE ILL-FATED BOAT THAT WAS WRECKED DURING A STORM OFF ST. ANNES ON JAN. 18TH 1906

A poignant postcard reminder of why the lifeboat station and volunteers were so badly needed to watch over the River Ribble and the rough Irish sea.

Church bells rang to herald Lord Ashton's gift of Ashton Gardens to the town in January 1914. The gardens had been originally established in 1875 as St George's Gardens. St Annes Land and Building Company had elaborate plans to develop the 12-acre site.   Ref No: SA14

Lord Ashton later gave a gift of £29,000 for the town's war memorial to be erected in Ashton Gardens. It was unveiled before 15,000 people including 800 ex-servicemen on parade.

Cash-flow problems later led to the gardens being part leased to Cartmells, a firm of florists and gardeners and also used as school playing fields. The gardens were offered for sale and the town was divided on whether St Annes Urban Council should buy. Lord Ashton then made a dramatic intervention – and paid £21,350 for the gardens and added a further £4,500 for expansion. The impressive fountain in Ashton Gardens commemorates Lord Ashton's gift to the town.

The Ashton Gardens institute, which has seen various uses over the years including a snooker hall and youth club headquarters.

Overlooked by impressive Porritt properties were the Ashton Gardens lawn tennis courts, which have long since disappeared.

The much-loved Ashton Theatre provided an all-year-round attraction with top stars taking part in summer season shows – until a massive blaze in September 1977. Despite many impassioned pleas and attempts the phoenix has still to rise from the ashes.

Ref No: SA15

St Annes was a seaside tonic for the elderly and saw the emergence of a number of convalescent homes – none closer to the sea than the Blackburn and District Home built in 1914.

Well-groomed staff in the patients' dining room of the Blackburn home, which today stands empty and sadly neglected among the sandhills on Clifton Drive North, St Annes.

St Annes Roman Baths opened in June 1916. A crowd of 4,000 attended the opening which included a procession from the Public Offices headed by mounted police and a band. Thousands visited the baths in their hey-day but the 1970s saw a sharp decline and they eventually closed in 1988. Not even a 2,000-name petition could keep them open.

Ref No: SA16

Diving boards and water chutes provided endless enjoyment for decades at the Roman Baths, hailed as unique in the north for having hot and cold filtered sea water, all year round.

Ref No: SA17

Happier days and a full house at the Open Air Baths and café as children play in the shallow end – which ran the full length of the pool.

There was plenty of entertainment with personality contests as well as bathing beauty competitions to attract entries as well as large crowds, as seen here in 1954. Crowds also enjoyed swimming galas, diving exhibitions and championships in the 1950s and the televised *It's A Knockout* from the 1960s.   Ref No: SA18

St Annes War Memorial Hospital pictured a year after it was opened by Lord Derby on Lytham St Annes Charter Day in 1922. The hospital was to have been built on a site in Headroomgate Road/Highbury Road until the St Annes Road East residence of Mr Thomas Bannister, Bannastre Holme, came onto the market for £10,000. The hospital closed in 1993. Ref No: SA19

ERNIE – the Electronic Random Indicator Equipment – during one of its early demonstrations. No one has done more to put St Annes on the map than the robot computer selector of Premium Bonds which was opened at the Bond and Stock offices in Moorland Road, St Annes by future Premier Harold McMillan in 1956. When ERNIE moved in and the Ministry of Agriculture moved out to Guildford, 11 Lytham St Annes churches appealed to parents not to let their children work for the `evil' Bonds Ref No: SA20

Old and the new – the Lytham St Annes YMCA in St Albans Road, first formed in 1922. The original wooden headquarters was opened by Princess Louise in 1924 and extended in 1948. This photograph was taken in September 1964 as the current HQ was being built. It was officially opened in March 1967 by the Duchess of Kent.   Ref No: SA21

The familiar landmark of St Thomas Parish Church, opened in 1900. As on most street corners a sign warns 'Chars A Bancs Prohibited', a practice which earned St Annes the name of 'the forbidden city'. Traders complained of jokes and jibes about the 13th commandment as these notices were dubbed. One motor coach driver was reported to have told his passengers 'pull your shoes off and hold your breath, we are about to pass through Lytham St Annes'.

For generations of youngsters from industrial inland towns, the St Annes sandhills provided endless fun and fascination. Many had never been to the seaside before. These were 'sand footballers' from the Wood Street camp.

In an age of Edwardian elegance, Promenade strollers remained heavily clothed throughout the hot summers, while on the sands Bernis and Davis sold `genuine' ice-cream from handcarts.

Seaside fun for children in 1907 meant paddling, fully clothed and with compulsory headwear. The Manchester writer of this card said: ``We like St Annes very much but it isn't as quiet as we expected.''

Birds eye view of the new St Annes Promenade as seen from the Majestic Hotel. In the foreground are the gardens of the Southdown Hydro, now the Town Hall, while landaus line up alongside the empty bandstand.

Cousin Freddie's White Coons entertained daily at his Cosy Corner – situated in a break between the sand-dunes between Lightburne Avenue and Riley Avenue.

Hats off to these holidaymakers in their marvellous seaside fashions in 1905. Large audiences were photographed in their finery as they watched Cousin Freddie's White Coons, to make seaside souvenirs.

Just like big brother Blackpool, St Annes tempted visitors to the beach with donkey rides and delicious ice cream.

The Promenade bandstand has always been a focal point for the crowds. Here Lady Ashton and members of the organising committee prepare to present prizes to donkey race winners.

Fashions may change but the Promenade crowds remain attracted as ever to stroll along the seafront as in this 1920s view.

The Oceandene, Lindum and Langcliffe Hotels loom over the seafront miniature golf course, created in 1934 and just as popular today with holidaymakers.

The miniature railway on St Annes Promenade remains a children's favourite to this day – although the platform's position appears to have changed. The café at the Fairhaven Road end of the gardens has since been completely rebuilt. The railway reopened in 1973 after an eight-year absence but a bid to extend the line to Fairhaven failed by one council vote, thanks to a 500-name protest petition.

The bathing vans of the early 1900s were replaced in popularity by the beach chalets. Families would hire the chalets – sometimes five years in advance – in order to use them for a summer season. In 1953 the full season cost would be £17 17s. About 80 wooden chalets were later rebuilt in brick but persistent storms and vandalism saw them lose their appeal and they were demolished in 1992.

A mechanical navvy scoops up shingle on St Annes beach between the Open Air Baths and Pier in 1934. Lytham St Annes Council spent £18,397 on turning six acres of shingle into the boating pool, building a sea wall and creating the miniature golf course.

Ref No: SA22

Start of work on the new boating pool on St Annes Promenade in 1934.

Ref No: SA23

Between the wars – a bustling Bank Holiday crowd on St Annes Promenade in August 1936 – with many uniforms in evidence.
Ref No: SA24

The boating pool was one of the final seafront attractions to be completed on the Promenade, but remains as popular as ever.
Ref No: SA25

A toy yacht and a boat hook meant hours of enjoyment for children at the boating pool surrounding the Promenade bandstand which by 1926 was no longer open to the elements but had been glassed in to provide a shelter. It was restored to its former Victorian glory in July 1982.

Seven miles of golden sands have provided an invigorating ride for generations of horse lovers, who maintain that the sea air and salt water is a good tonic for both horses and riders.

Ref No: SA26

Ice skating in the sandhills in January 1952. A pond on the landward side of Clifton Drive North – now known as the Lytham St Annes Nature Reserve – was a favourite play area for children. In the central background can be seen the last of the white-walled St Annes cottages, Cross Slack farm which stood on Old Links Golf Course.   Ref No: SA27

In the 1950s weekly sandcastle competitions on the beach attracted plenty of entries and admirers. Ansdell youngster Neville Holmes was the winner of this 1952 contest.   Ref No: SA28

St Annes had no need for two Promenade bandstands – so this earlier structure was removed.

The amphitheatre proved a popular venue for open air shows until it was finally given over for use as a children's paddling pool.

Soldiers get in shape, during World War One. Some 4,000 recruits trained in Lytham and St Annes.

Military activities such as drilling and trench digging were a common sight on the beach, the Pier forecourt and Promenade.

Bandsmen, no doubt sweltering in their heavy tunics, take time out to pose on the original St Annes bandstand, which has since been replaced by the children's paddling pool.

The elaborately-sculptured cast-iron water fountain, one of the original features of the Promenade Gardens, has retained its timeless fascination.

The meandering walk across stepping stones, bridge and beneath a waterfall which made up the Promenade Marine Gardens.

The well-manicured Promenade Marine Gardens were a sight to behold when finally completed and even included a small fenced weather station.

The creation of the Promenade Marine Gardens provided an attractive stroll for seaside visitors, pictured here braving the stepping stones in 1914.

Relaxing by the bandstand and lifeboat monument in 1905.

1 May 1922 was the day the two townships of Lytham and St Annes officially became one. The sound of lifeboat rockets and the ringing of church bells signalled the birth of the new borough. Big crowds defied the rain in St Annes Square.   Ref No: SA29

Town clerk Mr T. Bradley reads the official charter in St Annes Square. On the extreme right is Squire of Lytham Mr John Talbot Clifton.

The St Annes Pier story began in 1879, five years after the founder of St Annes, Rossendale businessman Elijah Hargreaves, formed St Annes Land and Building Company. The structure cost £18,000 to erect and was officially opened on 15 June 1885.

The domed Moorish-style Pavilion was added to the Pier in 1895 and had ornate decorations and carvings on walls, ceilings and stage which made holidaymakers gasp in admiration.

St Annes Pier would not have been the same without the Pier Orchestra. In 1925 the conductress was Miss Clarice Dunington, a solo violinist who in 1934 joined the Manchester Women's String Orchestra.

Plenty of laughter and smiles among this large open-air audience in deckchairs on St Annes Pier.

St Annes Pier in its 1960 hey-day with Moorish Pavilion, Floral Hall and amusement centre. Jack Storey was in summer season, Lionel Johns entertained with the Pier Orchestra and there were bars, restaurants, children's theatre and Standerwick coach trips from the forecourt. Ref No: SA30

Tragically the St Annes Pier Pavilion was destroyed by fire in July 1974. Forty firemen tackled the blaze as flames roared into the midnight sky and could be seen in Preston. Ref No: SA31

The skeletal remains of the Moorish Pavilion after the great blaze of 1974.   Ref No: SA32

The St Annes Pier Floral Hall opened in 1910 and was the setting for music concerts, eastern belly dancers and Tyrolean beer festivals. It was also gutted by fire in 1982 and the ruined seaward end of the pier was later demolished.

Ref No: SA33

The early days of spacious St Annes Square. Shops, some with glass verandahs, originally occupied just one side of St Annes Road West.

Before the arrival of the automobile, a landau approaches the Square from West Crescent in 1900. Large overhanging trees hide the St Annes Hotel as landaus await a fare near the railway station.   Ref No: SA34

The block setts of the tramway are much in evidence in this 1926 view of the developing St Annes Square. At the turn of the century part of St Annes Road West was called Hydro Gardens and consisted of many private residences with long gardens.

The plan of the new town of St Annes was laid out by Clifton Estates land agent Mr Thomas Fair.

Over the railway bridge to the Square for this landau as crowds gather on the Crescent in 1907.

Proud Crescent trader J.Stott, who gave his address as The Bridge, won first prize for his decorated horse and cart in the 1913 St Annes Carnival.

The first sign of traffic as pedestrians prepare to cross the Square in 1914. Between the flower beds on the north side, a band entertains the shoppers.

The rear of the Majestic Hotel dominates this 1950s view of the Square, lined with traffic and more recognisable with today.

North Crescent looking down the bridge towards Our Lady Star of the Sea RC Church in 1926. The scene has changed surprisingly little – only the names above the shop frontages have altered.

St Annes railway station pictured in 1930 after being extensively rebuilt just five years earlier. The view looks across the Crescent Gardens and a row of taxis can be seen awaiting the next steam train arrival.

An early St Annes Carnival Day parade. Between 1920 and 1945 they were known as Hospital Fete Days. Here a procession turns into Garden Street from bunting-decked St Annes Road West having just passed the civic party.

Parading the lifeboat – The horse-drawn vessel is pulled from its East Bank Road station along Clifton Drive South heading towards the Square.

Lytham St Annes first public transport service started in July 1895 with gas trams travelling at no more than six miles per hour between South Shore and St Annes which would take 40 minutes. The network finally closed with a ceremonial journey in 1937.

The end of an era as the last Lytham St Annes Corporation working horse retires in November 1954. Prince, aged 13, spent seven years on the streets of the town working from the highways depot in St David's Road North, St Annes, but finished his days working on a diary farm in North Wales. He is pictured with his driver Tom Dickinson – the author's grandfather – of Barton Road, St Annes.

Ref No: SA35

Fast fading into history – a Lytham St Annes Corporation bus built in 1960. First the trams disappeared and now the blue buses after being sold out to the much larger Blackpool Council operation.   Ref No: SA36

The jet age arrives with the construction of a new runway at Squires Gate airport in August 1953, which crossed Leach Lane. A temporary road to Division Lane was used to enable traffic to reach Blackpool across Marton Moss until the new Queensway was built.
Ref No: SA37

Golf put Lytham on the world map. Royal Lytham St Annes Golf Club is not especially old, being formed in 1886, but it is one Europe's most testing links courses – and a regular home of the British Open Golf Championship. Members originally met at the St Annes Hotel until the new clubhouse was started in 1896. During its construction materials had to be delivered by rough track, some of which were laid on railway sleepers. A bus service transported members from the hotel until the headquarters was finally completed in March 1898 when the Marquis of Lorne, later the Duke of Argyll, conducted the opening.   Ref No: SA38

Royal Lytham plays host to the Ryder Cup. Here two of the all-time greats Jack Nicklaus and Tom Watson study their shot for the USA team, in the 1977 competition. Princess Alexandria later presented the trophy to the victorious Americans.

Ref No: SA39

Four past winners of the famous British Open claret jug at Royal Lytham. Left: 1958, Peter Thomson. Centre top: 1974, Gary Player, bottom: 1963, Bob Charles. Right: 1969, Tony Jacklin, the first home-based player to win the British Open since Max Faulkner in 1951.   Ref Nos:SA 40/41/42/43

Seve Ballesteros who captured the prestigious British Open title at Royal Lytham in 1979 and again in 1988.
Ref No: SA44

Majestic by name, majestic by nature. This aerial view shows the giant hotel, standing in its vast grounds with tennis courts facing the Square. On the right is the Town Hall building and in the foreground St Annes Pier with a packed car park.

The vast expanse of some of the seven miles of beach can clearly be seen in this early aerial view which also shows little development outside the central square mile of St Annes. The Open Air Baths stand out on the foreshore.

This view of Queen Mary School from the early 1940s shows St Annes still developing with extensive building plots visible. Along King Edward Avenue and the Promenade long stretches of sandy wasteland were waiting for some of the finest St Annes residences to be built.

Cooksons Exhibition Bakery standing at the east end of Lytham Promenade with a slipway down to the River Ribble. The firm had humble beginnings as a small shop in Church Street, Preston, in 1886 when a Miss Hull (who later married a Mr E.Cookson) bought the concern for the sum of £35. The modern factory was built in 1930 and in 1954 it became part of Allied Bakeries.

The Ormerod Convalescent Home from the air surrounded by sandhills, where today there stands homes. Empty building plots abound on Clifton Drive North and in particular on Highbury Road West.

The Grand Hotel, surrounded by gardens, some of which have now been replaced by car parking areas. Also evident is the Kings Road garage which has since been demolished and the Marine Park Gardens in the foreground.

North Promenade seafront flats now stand alongside the original Porritt houses while substantial family homes grew up in Beach Road and adjoining streets in the early 20th century.

Ref No: SA45

The corner of Lowther Gardens facing Lowther Terrace with Lytham Green in the foreground. Beyond the early red-brick Georgian properties lies the tree-lined route of the railway line with the sprawl of the Lytham Hall estate and Guardian owned land in the background.

Ref No: SA46

147

The Fairhaven White Church – a landmark for miles around, surrounded on all sides by some of the most prestigious of Lytham St Annes property, some with a superb view across Granny's Bay. In the background can be seen Woodlands Road railway bridge and the eastern corner of the Royal Lytham golf course.

Ref No: SA47

Part of St Annes Promenade with the gardens and putting green in the foreground. The block between Kings Road and Hornby Road is a distinct mixture of old and new. Traditional hotels, new seafront flats and apartments and original mansions facing Clifton Drive South.

Ref No: SA48

Lytham Green from its eastern perimeter alongside the Land Registry where the Customs House once stood. Some of Lytham's finest properties overlook the Green.
Ref No: SA49

Lytham town centre looking down on Dicconson Terrace and Park Road with the glass verandah surrounding the Stringer store, one of the most distinctive features. In the background is the Wesleyan Chapel, better known as Park Street Methodist Church.
Ref No: SA50

St Annes Pier and forecourt facing the Majestic flats complex, where originally stood the finest of seafront hotels, the Majestic. All that remains today are the original gate posts. The corner of St Annes Square can be seen in the background.
Ref No: SA51

Wartime Prime Minister Winston Churchill, who led Britain throughout the conflict, visited the Fylde in 1946 when he was granted the Freedom of Blackpool. He is pictured signing the visitors book at the Council Chamber at the Town Hall, St Annes, watched by the Mayor Councillor J.Simpson JP.   Ref No: SA52

Swimsuits have changed a lot since comedy star Terry Thomas did the honours at the 1952 Miss Lytham St Annes Final – but maybe the British summer wasn't too hot as Terry kept his overcoat on!   Ref No: SA53

Look who's cleaning windows! – comedian George Formby is the man with the wash leather, busy cleaning his Rolls Royce and Jaguar with distinctive number plates outside his home Beryldene on the South Promenade, St Annes, in March 1958.

Yorkshire comedian, radio and television personality Wilfred Pickles and his wife Mabel holidayed in Lytham for more than ten years. He said Lytham never changed. ``That's the beauty of it. It's natural and restful and we can get away from all the bustle of work.''

Ref No: SA54

Blackpool FC players proudly display the FA Cup on a coach tour of the Fylde after their Wembley triumph in 1953. Stanley Matthews, who once owned a house on North Promenade, St Annes, is amongst them. Cheering crowds were out in force, pictured here outside the Town Hall, St Annes.
Ref No: SA55

Comedian Al Read (right) finds himself stuck in the stocks at a Lytham St Annes YMCA garden party in 1951. Many stars in Blackpool for the summer season preferred to stay in Lytham St Annes, where they could relax and unwind and, of course play golf. They included Val Doonican, Englebert Humperdinck and Cilla Black.
Ref No: SA56

Comedienne Hilda Baker (right) was guest of honour at Lytham Club Day and rose queen crowning ceremony in Lowther Gardens in 1956.

Ref No: SA57

The legendary Fred Perry (centre) opened the new St Annes Lawn Tennis Club headquarters in Avondale Road in 1963. He is flanked by Wimbledon winners Ken Rosewall and Rod Laver who played an exhibition match to mark the historic occasion.

Ref No: SA57

Comedienne Irene Handl was a VIP guest at the 7th Lytham St Annes scout fete.   Ref No: SA58

The Duke of Edinburgh opens Witchwood, Ansdell, in May 1954, accompanied by Mr Graeme Fallows of the Lytham St Annes Civic Society. The commemorative stone is on Blackpool Road, Ansdell, near the foot of Skew Bridge. The walk extends for about a mile finishing near Lytham railway station.   Ref No: SA59

In June 1974 Princess Anne attended a charity concert on the pier to celebrate the St Annes Land and Building Company's centenary – just a month before the Pavilion blaze.
Ref No: SA60

A youthful-looking Jimmy Saville was joined by Sir Fred Pontin on a visit to the Lytham St Annes YMCA in 1972.
Ref No: SA61

Master of mirth, Lancashire comedian Les Dawson was one of Lytham St Annes most famous adopted sons. After living in Bury for ten years he moved into a new £47,000 home, Garth in Islay Road, Lytham, in 1975. This photograph was taken by the outdoor swimming pool just a fortnight after the move. Les died in 1993 – a plaque commemorating the comedian, author and Water Rat has been placed on the house by Comic Heritage.

Ref No: SA62

Subscribers

Mr William John Aaron
Peter J Bamford
Mrs S M Boyes
Mrs W Bradley
Peter Bridge
C E Briggs
Miss M Broadhurst
Mr V Broadhurst
Girlie B'Tesh
Beryl Burnett
J E Burt
Stuart David Dewhurst
Mrs M P Dix
Robin & Beryl Donnelly
Andrew Firth
Brian & Elaine Firth
Robert Greenlees
Mr John Grime
Mrs K Halliday
Mr & Mrs D J Hammond
Mrs E R Hardman
Alan John Lees

Colin E MacLeod
A P Maitland
Gary Miller
Bryan J Palmer
Louisa Philpott
Mr Anthony D Roberts
Gordon Russell
Robert J Sanderson
Philip B Sanderson
Phylis M Sanderson
Mollie Schofield
Steve Singleton Snr
Bill Singleton
Eileen Singleton
Mrs Pamela I Smith
Alan Spencer MBE
Vera Todd
David Upton
Mr D M Walley
Philip Welsh
Fred Wild
N Edmund Yorke